DI
POSITIVE
THOUGHTS

A Pickleball Devotional
By Christy Largent

To request permissions, contact Christy Largent at christy@christylargent.com

ISBN: 9798875622069
Independently published.

Library of Congress Cataloging-in-Publication Data
Library of Congress Cataloging-in-Publication application has been submitted

First Paperback Edition December 2023

www.christylargent.com

For everyone eager to shine with the light of Jesus. May this little book encourage your heart and strengthen your walk both on and off the pickleball courts.

INTRODUCTION

I fell in love with Pickleball in December of 2019 while on a Christmas cruise to Central America. A woman had brought along her net, some paddles and balls, and I wanted to see what this game of Pickleball was all about. Playing full out, I tripped and landed belly-up on the deck. My kids were mortified. I was hooked!

For more than 20 years, I've taught mindset and communication skills in the business world. As a Christian since age 8, I've also read and studied the Bible in depth and know the deep connection God makes about how our thoughts inform our words which inform our actions.

This Christian Devotional, Dink Positive Thoughts came about as I got deeper into my Pickleball journey and realized how powerfully our thoughts on the court affected our play.

In 2 Corinthians 10:5 we're told to "take every thought captive" but that's easier said than done. One thing I've found helpful in this effort is to redirect my thoughts to better things.

Galatians 4:22-23 says "The fruit of the Spirit is love, joy peace, patience, kindness, goodness, faithfulness, gentleness, and self-control."

In this devotional, I wanted to let us dig deeper into these fruit of the Spirit, and see how we could be thinking on them and living them out more deeply, even as the Holy Spirit produces more of them in our lives.

I've set this up as a daily scripture, with a devotional thought, followed by a prayer and an affirmation with some room to take note of your thoughts. Hopefully, it will all work to help you "Dink Positive Thoughts" as you go.

See you on the Courts!
Christy

DAY 1 — LOVE

"Most important of all, continue to show deep love for each other, for love makes up for many of your faults."
—1 Peter 4:8 TLB

Most important of all...show deep love. This is so easy to say, yet can be so difficult to do. Especially when we are out on the courts. Our partner makes some dumb shots, they mistakenly call an out ball in, or they hog the whole court leaving you feeling left out.

I don't know about you, but when people act in "human" ways, I often want to scream. And act snotty. And get an attitude.

Instead, the next time we are tempted to get irritated with our partner, do the opposite. Speak words of encouragement. Cheer on their good shots. Physically, turn towards them at the end of the point rather than away from them.

In this way you will be putting love in action...and making up for many faults.

———

Dear God, help me to be your light shining love on the court regardless of the situation. Let me love like Jesus today.

Today I will look for and find ways to show love in action. I will shine the light of Jesus on the Pickleball courts and in my community.

DAY 2 — LOVE

"We know how much God loves us because we have felt his love and because we believe him when he tells us that he loves us dearly. God is love, and anyone who lives in love is living with God and God is living in him."
—1 John 4:16 TLB

Do you remember the first time you held your child in your arms? That overwhelming sense of love. That all-encompassing awareness that this child was yours. And you were filled with...love.

Do you believe God when he tells you how much he loves you? It's truly knowing his love for us that allows us to love others.

Living in the love of God means living out his love for others every day. Simple acts like picking up your partner so she doesn't have to drive, dropping off flowers to a sick friend, or sending a "thinking of you" card are all easy ways to say I love you.

If you struggle with this, remind yourself of how much HE loves you. And then let yourself channel that love to others.

Dearest God, today, let me be a vessel of your love to those around me. Let me be the physical example of your love to someone today.

Because God loved me first, I can love others in ways that help them feel loved by God.

_____

_____

_____

_____

_____

_____

_____

_____

_____

_____

_____

_____

_____

_____

_____

DAY 3 — LOVE

"Let all that you do be done in love."
—1 Corinthians 16:14 ESV

A former pastor of mine used to say, "All means all, that's all all means." When it comes to acting in love, the Bible is pretty clear. Let's act lovingly. All the time. Be loving in your actions at home, at work, and on the Pickleball courts.

What does love look like on the courts?

Playing honestly, giving the benefit of the doubt, encouraging your partner, cheering your opponents' good shots, tapping paddles no matter the score at the end of the game.

It doesn't have to be difficult to act lovingly. And it will shine Jesus on the court as brightly as the noon-day sun when we do it.

Father, help me act lovingly every day in every way. Let me drop my ego, pride and fear and channel your love as a light in this dark world.

I am a loving person who finds every opportunity to spread love through my words and actions.

_____

_____

_____

_____

_____

_____

_____

_____

_____

_____

_____

_____

_____

_____

DAY 4 — LOVE

"And may the Lord make you increase and abound in love for one another and for all, as we do for you."
—1 Thessalonians 3:12 ESV

I just don't like this one lady I play with in open play. Honestly. She's always negative and when she's my partner, I get all nervous as every mistake I make is received with a sigh or an unhappy look.

But one day I overheard her talking with another player about her home situation and wow, did I get a perspective shift.

Her husband is ill, her kids are estranged and she's really quite alone. Pickleball is her only "escape" all week long.

And I was reminded how important it is to be loving no matter how the other person is behaving.

This verse reminds us we don't have to do it on our own. May the LORD make you increase and abound in Love...

And that makes me happy. Because I know without a shadow of a doubt that if I ask, he will help me be positive and encouraging and a light of love for this sad and lonely woman.

And when I think of it this way, I realize that shining the light of Jesus on this lady may be the literal bright spot in a dark time in her life. And that's a privilege.

———

Oh Jesus, help me increase and abound in love for others. Help me see others as you see them. Help me be the light of love in this dark world.

It's my privilege to shine the light of Jesus on the court and off. I get to be the light in this dark world.

_____

_____

_____

_____

_____

_____

_____

_____

_____

_____

_____

_____

_____

_____

_____

DAY 5 — JOY

"Rejoice in the Lord always: and again I say, Rejoice!"
—Philippians 4:4 KJV

I just love this verse. It's like a secret we Christians can tap into anytime and anywhere.

The verse reminds us to find our joy in the Lord. Not in our circumstances or surroundings. Not in the play of our partner or whether we win or lose on the court. Our joy comes from rejoicing in the Lord.

He is the only one who is consistently all good all the time. We can always count on him, trust him, and rely on him.

We just need to set our minds to seek the good to be found. Turn your mind to finding evidence of all the good all around, all the time. And in this way, we can rejoice in the Lord, which is always gratitude-inducing. And when we are filled with gratitude the joy follows. Rejoice in the Lord!

———

Dear Lord, show me how to find the good. Show me how to find you in every situation so that I'm drawn to rejoice in you. Help me feel the deep abiding joy that comes from you.

I am a joyful person who finds the good in even the most difficult situations.

DAY 6 — JOY

"These things I have spoken to you, that my joy may be in you and that your joy may be full."
—John 15:11 ESV

What do you think the joy of Jesus was like? Can you even imagine how his perfect heart was often filled to the brim with the joy of life and how that joy spilled out and over everyone around him? He was joy-filled and in this verse, he tells us that our joy can also be full.

Sometimes on the courts, it's easy to be full of joy. The long point that ends with everyone gasping and laughing...Your perfect ace serve that surprises both you and your opponent.

It's the difficult moments that threaten to steal our joy. The irritation at a disengaged partner...The shots you miss...The easy points squandered.

Getting irritated or frustrated is as normal and natural a part of playing as the joy-filled moments.

The key is to feel the difficult feelings...then LET THEM GO. Don't hold on to them, nurse them and let them bring you and everyone else down.

As Christians, we know our joy is a spark. A gift from God we can use for our own happiness as well as the happiness of others.

Dear Lord, when the difficult feelings come, help me to feel them, then let them go, so I can return to the joy of my salvation and let that joy radiate out to everyone around me.

*Emotions are a good thing. I feel them all,
process them and then choose to let the joy of the
Lord rise up and flow over.*

_____

_____

_____

_____

_____

_____

_____

_____

_____

_____

_____

_____

_____

_____

_____

_____

DAY 7 — JOY

*"Rejoice with those who rejoice, weep with those
who weep."*
—Romans 12:15 ESV

Don't you just love it when you have a really good point?
You know, it's not just a serve, return, and into the net. It's
a good point. With dropping and driving and dinking and
you get balls you had no idea you could get and the whole
point ends with someone making an incredible shot and
you all cheer together?

It's a lot easier to rejoice together after that point than at
the end of the game when I lose.

Just being honest here. I often find it difficult to rejoice
with my opponent after I've lost. But the Bible is pretty
clear here. We get to do both with others in our life. We get
to celebrate and cry together.

God made us for community, and rejoicing and weeping
are all part of the human condition.

So the next time you lose, ask God to help you rejoice
with the winning team. We show the love of Jesus when we
add to their joy by rejoicing.

---

*Dear God, help me to recognize my emotions so that
when I am sad with a loss, I'm able to feel that sadness
(or anger) and then let it go (breathe it out) so that I'm
able to give joy back by rejoicing with my opponent.*

I'm so thankful I get to play pickleball. Win or lose, it's all a blessing.

DAY 8 — PEACE

"Let the peace of Christ rule in your hearts, since as members of one body you were called to peace. And be thankful."
—Colossians 3:15 NIV

Are you thankful? It's funny how Paul throws this little aside in there at the end of his suggestions for having peace. As we all know, anxiety is at an all-time high. And it's the peace of Christ that brings us relief from that anxiety.

What is often missing in the conversation though, is that last sentence. "And be thankful."

Playing Pickleball gives us many reasons to be thankful. We are thankful for our health, for our friends, for a fun sport where we can have fun and just play.

Yet I often see players caught up with all the things that are wrong, rather than focusing on what's right.

It's by focusing on what's right, with gratitude, and by acknowledging that it's Christ who gives us lasting peace, that we can fully be who we are called to be.

Dearest God, Please give me the peace that passes all understanding as I let your peace rule in my heart. Remind me to be thankful for all of the amazing things you have given me. Thank you for being an abundant, peace-giving, and generous God.

I am a thankful person and daily I invite Christ to rule my heart with his peace that passes all understanding.

DAY 9 — PEACE

"Blessed are the peacemakers, for they will be called children of God."
—Matthew 5:9 NIV

One of my favorite ladies on the court is Annie. She is always calm and gentle. I love playing with her because she brings that spirit of peace with her onto the court. Just being around her settles me down.

I know that no matter the outcome, Annie is a peacemaker. When we are in a game with crazy people, Annie always smiles and laughs and helps me stay present in the moment, enjoying it all.

And her peace travels across the net too. I notice that even her opponents recognize and appreciate her peaceful presence.

Can you be a peacemaker? Can you answer any provocation with a peaceful response? Blessings await us as we commit to becoming a peacemaker.

———

Dear Father, Thank you that you sent Jesus to bring us peace. You are the ultimate peacemaker and help me to reflect you in that way as well. Remind me to be open to your Spirit's leading on the court and off to help me be a peacemaker too.

*I am a peacemaker. I let the love of Christ fill me
up so I radiate peace in every situation.*

DAY 10 — PATIENCE

"And let us not grow weary of doing good, for in due season we will reap, if we do not give up."
—Galatians 6:9 ESV

I drill twice a week with a coach. Over and over and over we hit hundreds of dinks, drops, and drives. With every day of practice and focus on the fundamentals, I'm getting a little bit better.

To be honest, I don't always want to drill. But I started Pickleball with very, little racquet sport background, so since I want to improve, I have a lot of work to do.

Some days it seems like I'm not making any progress at all. But then other days I surprise myself with my improved skills.

It's the same with our faith walk. Paul urges us to "not grow weary in doing good." That tells me the Galatians were doing good, but were getting tired of it because they just couldn't see anything happening.

Paul's encouragement to them... "at the proper time you'll see results..." all hinges on them not giving up. Just keep at it he says. And with us - whether on the court or in our homes, just keep at it. And at the proper time, we'll reap the harvest.

Dear Lord, please help me to stick with it. When I feel like quitting, encourage me to stay the course. Doing good as I'm able with your power, help me to love others and to do good, even when I don't see results.

I'm a person who sticks with what I've started. I keep doing good. I keep practicing. And I leave the results up to God.

DAY 11 — PATIENCE

*"But if we hope for what we do not see, we wait for it
with patience."*
—Romans 8:25 ESV

Paul is talking about our future hope, and waiting for it with patience. You see, God has done all the work for us already. And that's why we can wait with patience. He already has it all in hand.

Often I find myself impatient with myself and others in many areas, and especially on the Pickleball court. I watch the Pros and am amazed at their speed, patience and intuitive understanding of the game. Then I get on the court and miss a dink, or hit it into the net, or long, and I get so impatient. Why can't I play my game the way I see it in my head?

God understands our impatience. He understands we will always want things to happen right away. He understands.

So he reminds us to hope for the future (with faith) and wait for it with patience. Whether it's for our game to improve, or for our future time with God in heaven, we can learn to wait with patience.

———

Dearest God, thank you for being an all-knowing and patient God. Thank you for your completed work on the cross. Thank you we can wait for our future hope with patience, knowing you have it all prepared already. Help me to patiently trust you and wait expectantly for your perfect timing in all things in my life.

*God's timing is perfect and each day I'm learning
to wait with patience for his perfect plan.*

DAY 12 — PATIENCE

"Finishing is better than starting! Patience is better than pride!"
—Ecclesiastes 7:8 TLB

When I played Pickleball for the first time, I was on a ship in the middle of the Caribbean, and some lady had brought her net, balls and some paddles with her. She set up on the upper deck, and I had my first experience with the game that would become my passion.

It's so easy to start new things, especially Pickleball. The excitement! The challenge! The possibilities! The fun!

Starting is always easier than sticking with it through to the finish though. The problem is that you can't experience the delight of a job well done unless you stick with it.

You won't increase your Pickleball skills unless you persevere and work on your game. Day in and day out, putting in the work to get stronger, more flexible, faster. This is hard work and it would be easy to stop doing it and just rest on your natural abilities.

But that would be your pride talking. Instead, patiently put in the work and you will reap the reward of improvement.

———

Father, help me to be a person of perseverance. To stick with what you have called me to until I see the reward of a job well done. Help me to be a finisher for your glory.

I start and finish the things God has called me to do. I stick with it until I can enjoy the fruit of my labors.

_____

_____

_____

_____

_____

_____

_____

_____

_____

_____

_____

_____

_____

_____

DAY 13 — KINDNESS

"Love is patient, love is kind. It does not envy, it does not boast, it is not proud."
—1 Corinthians 13:4 NIV

We have a chance to be kind every single time we play Pickleball. Think about when your partner keeps hitting her returns out. There's a chance to be kind. Or when you're playing with a newbie. Many chances to be kind to them. Or when your opponent makes questionable outcalls over and over again. Another perfect opportunity for kindness.

For most of us, kindness doesn't come naturally. We like to be "right" and our egos often prompt us to behave pridefully.

I think our time on the courts is a perfect time to show the love of Jesus to a hurting world by being kind.

Think of when someone was kind to you. You may or may not have deserved it, but my guess is you were blessed by their kindness.

You can do the same. Turn from pride and be kind.

———

Dearest God, Help me to be kind. Convict me when I'm being prideful and egocentric. Remind me that kindness comes from you first, and that we have the blessing of passing it on. Let me share kindness each and every day.

I look for ways to bless others with kindness every day. When I am kind, I'm a gift of God's light to a dark and wounded world.

_____

_____

_____

_____

_____

_____

_____

_____

_____

_____

_____

_____

_____

DAY 14 — KINDNESS

*"Therefore, as God's chosen people, holy and dearly
loved, clothe yourselves with compassion, kindness,
humility, gentleness and patience."*
—Colossians 3:12 NIV

In this verse Paul combines kindness with compassion,
humility, gentleness and patience. Because when we are
kind, we are usually acting with compassion. We are humble, gentle and we are patient.

Paul says to "clothe" ourselves in these things. This
means we intentionally cover ourselves in a beautiful cloak
of these behaviors.

As you can see from the first part of the verse, we can
do this because we are God's chosen people. We don't do
it from our own strength but from the strength of the indwelling Holy Spirit.

The next time you play Pickleball, as you do your stretches and warmups, breathe in deeply and picture yourself
pulling on a cloak of these elements.

And when you hit the court, you'll be prepared to move in
the grace of kindness, compassion, humility, gentleness and
patience. And you'll be a true picture of Christ in action.

---

*Dear God, thank you that you've given me the indwelling
power of the Holy Spirit. Help me to remember to "cloak
up" and be ready to move in your grace.*

I'm filled with the Holy Spirit and he has given
me everything I need to be a reflection of Christ.

_____

_____

_____

_____

_____

_____

_____

_____

_____

_____

_____

_____

_____

_____

_____

_____

DAY 15 — GOODNESS

"Turn away from evil and do good; seek peace and pursue it."
—Psalm 34:14 ESV

Isn't it interesting that seeking peace comes after turning from evil? We know the heart is deceitful, desperately wicked and who can know it (Jeremiah 17:9), so it's only the indwelling Holy Spirit that allows us to turn from evil.

To be honest, I see my sin nature come out on the Pickleball court. The ball hits on the outside edge of the line and I call it out. I see my partner's foot touch the kitchen line, and I say nothing. The score is confused and I give myself the advantage.

I don't do these things often, but I'm convicted when I do. I want to follow this directive and turn from evil. Then I'll be the person who does good (not evil) and I'll be pursuing peace with my good actions.

Let's follow the prompting of the Holy Spirit and choose to turn from evil and do good. That's when His light will shine through us.

Lord, help me turn from evil. Give me the prompting to choose the right thing over the easy or beneficial to me. Help me be a person of integrity who makes right choices of goodness. Nudge me to be a person who pursues peace.

I am a person after God's own heart and I love to choose the right thing over the easy thing. I look for and pursue peace.

DAY 16 — GOODNESS

"I remain confident of this, I will see the goodness of the Lord in the land of the living."
—Psalm 27:13 NIV

My Grandmother was born in 1900 and lived until she was a month shy of 100 years old. She had a lot of funny sayings and she used one of them often when she would call and ask, "Are you still in the land of the living?"

When I saw this verse, it made me smile and think of Nana. And for us, we can smile and be confident that we WILL see the goodness of the Lord while we live.

We are so fortunate to have the game of Pickleball. It's like a joy generator for us every time we play.

We get to move our body and be active and make new friends and laugh and have fun. What a blessing!

The next time we play, let's take a moment to remember that we can see the goodness of the Lord as we get to experience this fantastic sport. It's a little gift from Him, reminding us that there is lots and lots of goodness in the land of the living.

———————

Dear Lord, please remind me to find the good every day. And especially when I'm playing, help me remember this is one of your good blessings, and let me be thankful for it.

There is always goodness to be found in the land of the living.

DAY 17 — GOODNESS

"Therefore, as we have opportunity, let us do good to all people."
—Galatians 6:10a NIV

Susie came to the courts with her bag full of colorful bag tags made of mini Pickleballs. She had taken her time and money to create these cute gifts and she thoughtfully made one for each of us.

Tom gets to the courts early, so he can make sure all the nets are properly set up, and the courts are clear and ready for play. He generously gives of his time to make sure the Pickleball experience is great for everyone.

These friends are living out the directive of "let us do good to all people." They are going beyond the expected and looking for the opportunity to do good.

I must admit, I often forget to actually look for the opportunity to do good. It's easy to go along without thought for others, but what a blessing when we follow Paul's exhortation and look for ways to do good.

———

Dearest God, please help me get my eyes off myself and look for opportunities to do good to others around me. Let me be a giver of good and a bringer of joy.

I'm a person who looks for and sees opportunities to do good. I seek out ways to do good for others every single day.

DAY 18 — GOODNESS

" Let your light so shine before men, that they may see your good works and give glory to your Father who is in heaven."
—Matthew 5:16 RSV

A favorite song from the movie Moana is "Shiny," where the giant crab sings about his love of being shiny. As Christians, we are to be shiny too. But not from jewels or achievements. Shiny with the light of Christ.

We want to be people who shine for Christ. Letting his light radiate out of us each day. We are indwelt with the Holy Spirit, so His light is inside of us already.

It's our good deeds (that He enables) that show up as a light in this dark world.

On the court our good deeds could look like befriending new (or shy) players. Offering to stay and put the nets away when court time is over. Or volunteering in the myriad of ways available for most Pickleball programs.

And remembering why we want to shine for Jesus...so that unbelievers will see that light, and be drawn to God through us.

Dear God, help me to shine with the light of you. Not to seek the world's shiny objects, but to know that my good deeds done for your glory are all the shine I'm called to do and be.

*I radiate the love of Jesus to everyone I meet
with simple acts of good deeds.*

DAY 19 — FAITHFULNESS

"Let love and faithfulness never leave you; bind them around your neck, write them on the tablet of your own heart."
—Proverbs 3:3 NIV

How do we write love and faithfulness on our hearts? How do we become a person bound up with love and faithfulness?

What does it look like to be a person of love and faithfulness?

Here are some ideas:

- Have an encouraging word ready for other players while you're waiting to play.
- Be constantly positive with your partner like Pickleball Pro Vivienne David, who always encourages her partner no matter what the score.
- Turn towards your partner after each point, no matter win or lose the point.
- Show up on time or early for scheduled play.
- Give it your all, no matter how you feel that day.

These are simple behaviors, but I believe they show both love and faithfulness and are a testimony to Christ in us.

Dear Lord, help me to be a person of love and faithfulness. Help me to be kind, generous, loving, and thoughtful to those I play with so that I can be a great testimony for you today.

I'm a person who is loving and faithful. People can count on me to bring positivity and joy every day.

DAY 20 — FAITHFULNESS

"But the Lord is faithful, and he will strengthen you and protect you from the evil one."
—2 Thessalonians 3:3 NIV

Last week I was supposed to play with a group of women. All 4 of us agreed to the date and time, but when we got to the courts to play, only 3 of us showed up. To be honest, it was frustrating as we had to scramble to find a 4th, and our playtime was cut down by the disruption.

As I was reading this verse, I was a bit convicted. You see, I had been pretty upset at the friend who didn't show up. She didn't text, call or anything, but just ghosted us all.

I self-righteously thought, "How inconsiderate! How flakey! How unreliable!"

And yet...I must admit that sometimes I'm the flakey one.

Aren't you glad you can rely on the One who is always faithful? He will never let us down. And, he strengthens us and protects us even when we don't deserve it.

Dear loving God, thank you for always being faithful. Thank you that I can always count on you to love, strengthen, and protect me. Today, help me to show the same faithfulness and generosity to others.

Day by day, little by little, I am becoming a more faithful person and a truer reflection of Christ.

_____

_____

_____

_____

_____

_____

_____

_____

_____

_____

_____

_____

_____

_____

_____

DAY 21 — FAITHFULNESS

"Let us hold unswervingly to the hope we profess, for he who promises is faithful."
—Hebrews 10:23 NIV

Every day before I get on the courts, I take a moment and visualize how I want to play. I take a deep breath and call to mind one of my favorite Pickleball Pros, Callie Jo Smith, and picture myself playing as her, with a perfect third shot drop, a powerful drive, and the always-ready split-step. And then I go out on the court.

Ahhhhhh, hope springs eternal.

Day in and out I hold to the hope I will be able to apply all the drills, strength training, agility skills and film I'm incorporating into my daily activities.

And pretty much, daily, I'm disappointed.

Yes, my hope springs eternal that I will become an amazing player. But to be honest, I think that hope is slightly misplaced.

How much better to hope in the Lord. The hope we profess is in a faithful and perfect God who will always deliver on his promises. Let us hold unswervingly to that best hope.

———

Dear God, Thank you for being a faithful God, in whom I can unswervingly hope. Please remind me to keep my hope in the right things, namely you and your purpose in my life. Let me be a hope bringer for others.

My actions show I have true hope in an all-wise,
all-knowing, and all-loving God.

_____

_____

_____

_____

_____

_____

_____

_____

_____

_____

_____

_____

_____

_____

DAY 22 — GENTLENESS

"Be completely humble and gentle; be patient, bearing with one another in love."
—Ephesians 4:2 NIV

How do we bear with one another in love? What does it look like in action when we are playing with our league team week in and out and have to deal with all the various personalities? MaryJo who talks incessantly. Tiffany who constantly complains. Debra who is so competitive she completely falls apart when she loses.

Bearing with one another in love requires first that we humble ourselves (I'm really not all that perfect myself) and then be gentle, and then we can bear with each other in love.

When my teammate's behavior is getting on my last nerve, I can take a deep breath and remind myself "gentle."

Then I remind myself that MaryJo is just lonely since her husband died, Tiffany is having a difficult time with her adult kids and Debra had a father who told her she was only valuable when she achieved, and then I'm able to find love for these dear women.

Dear Lord, Help me to be humble, to let go of my judgments and patiently bear with those in my life. Help me love them well, bearing with all their imperfections, and encouraging them on all the more.

I'm a humble, gentle person. I show unconditional love to those I'm around.

DAY 23 — GENTLENESS

"Speak evil of no one, avoid quarreling, be gentle, and
show perfect courtesy toward all people."
—Titus 3:2 ESV

I think we need this verse on a plaque outside every pickleball court and pinned to the top of every Facebook group! Just imagine...how much content and behavior would be banned!

Seriously, what a great admonition for us all. As Christians, we need to be different from the world, and this verse outlines a simple way to differentiate.

What if we spoke only good things, got along with everyone, and were extremely courteous to all? I think that would be significant enough that others would notice.

I admit I often fall short. (Why is it that gossip sometimes actually feels good?) But I can turn around (repent) and act a better way instead. Imagine if we all did this on our courts today? We would be tangibly glorifying God and showing what's possible with Christ.

———

Dearest God, Please help me to be the kind of person
who speaks only good, is known for my gentleness, and
is unfailingly courteous. All this is only possible with
your help. Please help me for your glory.

*I'm a blessing to others every day with the words
I speak and the way I act.*

DAY 24 — GENTLENESS

"Let your gentleness be evident to all, the Lord is near."
—Philippians 4:5 NIV

On the Pickleball courts are a funny place to think about being gentle. Sometimes the word gentle might imply weak or passive. But the definition of gentleness actually includes being calm, kind, and careful.

I'd love to play with a partner who is calm, kind, and careful! I'd love to BE the partner who is calm, kind, and careful.

The last part of the verse gives us the answer as to how we can be this way. It's because the Lord is near. And if we have the indwelling Holy Spirit, we just need to ask for his help so that we can act accordingly.

Let's be the person on the court known for our gentleness. The Pro Vivienne David comes to mind (again.) She lives gentleness out at the highest levels and with the Lord's help, we can too.

Dear God, help me to remember to ask for help so I can be calm, kind and careful. Help me act out of gentleness rather than react from fear and with frantic anxiety. Thank you that you are always near.

I'm known for being calm, kind, and careful, and in this way I'm gentle.

DAY 25 — GENTLENESS

*"A gentle answer turns away wrath, but a harsh word
stirs up anger."*
—Proverbs 15:1 NIV

Did you know that we learned how to respond to anger
when we were just children?

Maybe you learned that when someone was angry with
you, you had to get angrier right back. Or when you were
criticized by a parent, you learned they would back off when
you reacted in anger. These angry reactions were primarily
your own body trying to help you by using anger as a protection
mechanism from the triggered fight or flight reaction.

The key as an adult, is to learn how to take care of your
nervous system so it's not as "trigger happy" as it was before.
We can get enough sleep, and start the day with deep
breathing, and have a devotion and prayer time. We can
journal our feelings and reactions so we become more
aware of what our triggers are, so we're not surprised.

Developing this skill will help on the court too, as with
practice you will be more than capable of giving a gentle
answer in reaction to anger.

---

*Dear God, help me recognize my trigger areas so that
I can practice healthy responses and be sensitive to
when I'm reacting rather than responding. Thank you
that you gave my body this protection system, and help
me to steward it well.*

I'm good at responding in gentleness rather than reacting in anger.

DAY 26 — SELF CONTROL

"A man without self-control is like a city broken into and left without walls."
—Proverbs 25:28 ESV

Being self-controlled in Pickleball is really important. Getting to the net and hitting dink after dink without impatiently speeding up, is a skill learned and developed.

The #1 professional Pickleball player in the world, Ben Johns, shows us self-control week in and week out. His emotions contained, attention focused solely on the game at hand, he just stays laser-focused and intense.

I most certainly will never be a Ben Johns in my level of skill. But I can take a page from his game, and apply his self-control to my game.

The next time I'm tempted to speed up unnecessarily, I'll take a breath and stay slow. And when my opponent makes a nasty comment or my partner exhibits frustration, I'll simply breathe in, find my calm, and smile, staying focused on the game at hand.

How can you build your self-control the next time you're tempted?

Dear Lord, Help me to be self-controlled. Help me be patient and filled with calm. Show me ways to stay peaceful and in control, even when I want to scream. Thanks for always understanding and helping me find a way.

I am a patient and self-controlled person.

DAY 27 — SELF CONTROL

"Whoever is slow to anger is better than the mighty, and he who rules his spirit than he who takes a city."
—Proverbs 16:32 ESV

I held my breath as he threw his paddle.

I had a feeling that was coming because the entire game, my (open play) partner had been getting angrier and angrier with each lost point.

First it was the swearing under his breath. Then it was the angry looks and hitting himself on the leg with his paddle.

So when we lost the game, and he threw his paddle, I really wasn't that surprised.

But it kind of spoiled the fun of the game.

What kind of person do you want to be? Slow to anger and ruling your spirit or the other? We shine brighter for Christ when we control our emotions on the court. Let's be the person on the courts who brings laughter and joy.

———————

Dear God, empower me to be a person of peace and calm. Take away my quick temper and rash reactions. Help me show your grace and peace to everyone I play with, for your glory.

I am a slow-to-anger and peaceful person both on and off the Pickleball court.

DAY 28 — SELF CONTROL

"A fool gives full vent to his spirit, but a wise man quietly holds it back."
—Proverbs 29:11 ESV

You've seen those players who go crazy point after point. Whether they are winning or losing the point, they either celebrate or stress out in a wild way.

I might be guilty of this - mainly on the celebrating part. I've been known to scream out with joy after a shot well hit.

And this verse reminds me maybe I need to reel it in a bit. "Full vent to his spirit" is quite an expression.

The word used for holding back is the Hebrew word **shabach**, which means "to soothe or to still" something.

Thinking about how my over-the-top emotional outburst (even when it's positive) can offend or irritate the other players on the court, makes me think twice about "giving full vent" to my emotions.

Next time, I think I'll choose wisdom and celebrate with moderation. Will you join me?

———————

Oh Lord, help me to be more considerate about how my emotional expressions might affect those around me. I want to glorify you in all places, including on the Pickleball courts, so help me play with wisdom and consideration for others.

I'm glad I can be fully me and fully self-controlled and respectful at the same time.

DAY 29 — ANXIETY

"Do not be anxious about anything, but in everything, by prayer and supplication with thanksgiving, let your requests be made known unto God. And the peace of God, which passes all understanding, will guard your hearts and minds in Christ Jesus."
—Philippians 4:6-7 ESV

These days, all kinds of things trigger anxiety. Pickleball should be one area where we don't have anxiety, but for most of us, it will show up there as well.

This verse shows us the best way to overcome that anxiety, no matter the situation. It starts with gratitude.

The next time you're walking on the court and feel that anxiety creeping in, take a deep breath, then list off in your head all the things you have to be thankful for in the moment.

Just being healthy enough to be on the court is a great place to start! Follow that with gratitude for your partner, your facility, your friends and of course your cute outfit!

Soon, the anxiety will be gone and you'll be able to enjoy a lovely time of Pickleball.

———

Dear Lord, thank you for all the blessings you have given me. Help me to focus on those things rather than the things I'm anxious about. Let me leave the anxiety with you, and accept the peace you long to give.

*I'm good at handing over my anxiety to the Lord,
and at finding lots of things to be thankful for,
because I'm a thankful person.*

DAY 30 — BLESSING

"And God is able to bless you abundantly, so that in all things at all times, having all that you need, you will abound in every good work."
—2 Corinthians 9:8 NIV

We *get* to do good work for the Lord. Whether that "work" is on the Pickleball court or at our desk, we have the great privilege of doing work that glorifies God.

Interestingly, our work follows because God has blessed us abundantly; all the time, giving us all that we need.

The next time we head out for a game, let's remember that our ability to play is a blessing from God. A big, huge, wonderful gift. And that's not our only blessing, He gives us exactly the ones we need for us to do the work he has given us to do.

Take a moment and think about how this is true in your life today. What blessings do you have that allow you to do the work you do? No matter your stage of life, if you're still breathing, then God is still blessing you for work.

———

Thank you for your abundant blessings. Thank you that you created me for a purpose. Help me to recognize and acknowledge your blessings every day, and to honor you with my time and efforts.

I'm a thankful person and I live a life of gratitude, honoring God with my work.

AFFIRMATIONS

Today I will look for and find ways to show love in action. I will shine the light of Jesus on the Pickleball courts and in my community.

Because God loved me first, I can love others in ways that help them feel loved by God.

I am a loving person who finds every opportunity to spread love through my words and actions.

It's my privilege to shine the light of Jesus on the court and off. I get to be the light in this dark world.

I am a joyful person who finds the good in even the most difficult situations.

Emotions are a good thing. I feel them all, process them, and then choose to let the joy of the Lord rise up and flow over.

I'm so thankful I get to play pickleball. Win or lose, it's all a blessing.

I am a thankful person and daily I invite Christ to rule my heart with his peace that passes all understanding.

I am a peacemaker. I let the love of Christ fill me up so I radiate peace in every situation.

I'm a person who sticks with what I've started. I keep doing good. I keep practicing. And I leave the results up to God.

God's timing is perfect and each day I'm learning to wait with patience for his perfect plan.

I start and finish the things God has called me to do. I stick with it until I can enjoy the fruit of my labors.

I look for ways to bless others with kindness every day. When I am kind, I'm a gift of God's light to a dark and wounded world.

I'm filled with the Holy Spirit and he has given me everything I need to be a reflection of Christ.

I am a person after God's own heart and I love to choose the right thing over the easy thing. I look for and pursue peace.

There is always goodness to be found in the land of the living.

I'm a person who looks for and sees opportunities to do good. I seek out ways to do good for others every single day.

I radiate the love of Jesus to everyone I meet with simple acts of good deeds.

I'm a person who is loving and faithful. People can count

on me to bring positivity and joy every day.

Day by day, little by little, I am becoming a more faithful person and a truer reflection of Christ.

My actions show I have true hope in an all-wise, all-knowing, and all-loving God.

I'm a humble, gentle person. I show unconditional love to those I'm around.

I'm a blessing to others every day with the words I speak and the way I act.

I'm known for being calm, kind, and careful, and in this way I'm gentle.

I'm good at responding in gentleness rather than reacting in anger.

I am a patient and self-controlled person.

I am a slow-to-anger and peaceful person both on and off the Pickleball court.

I'm glad I can be fully me and fully self-controlled and respectful at the same time.

I'm good at handing over my anxiety to the Lord, and at finding lots of things to be thankful for, because I'm a thankful person.

I'm a thankful person and I live a life of gratitude, honoring God with my work.

My habit is to make the things I think about and the things I say acceptable to God.

SCRIPTURE INDEX

Hebrews

1 Peter

1 John

ABOUT THE AUTHOR

Christy Largent, a professional speaker turned pickleball addict, has over 20 years of expertise teaching communication, mindset and midlife skills. After falling in love with pickleball, she founded the Christian Pickleball Collective and developed The Pickleball Evangelism System. You can follow her on Instagram @christylargent and YouTube @theChristyLargent for the latest, and stay connected through her Pickleball Conversations podcast. You can also find more information at www.christylargent.com

Follow Christy on:
Instagram: @christylargent
Instagram: @christianpickleballcollective
YouTube: @thechristylargent
www.christylargent.com

I hope you enjoyed this book and you're even more confident so you can "Dink Positive Thoughts" both on and off the court. If you did, would you would be so kind as to leave a review?

Reviews are how Amazon ranks books and how other people will find the book. I'd appreciate it so much and thank you in advance! It means the world to me!

–Christy